www.finishinglinepress.com

Straight Jacket

Sept 2019

Dear Darby,
Thank you so much for
your support and fellowship.
I will hope these poems
will mean something to you.
Mad Love,
Jessica ♡

poems by

Jessica Lowell Mason

Finishing Line Press
Georgetown, Kentucky

Straight Jacket

Copyright © 2019 by Jessica Lowell Mason
ISBN 978-1-63534-997-9 First Edition
All rights reserved under International and Pan-American Copyright Conventions.
No part of this book may be reproduced in any manner whatsoever without written
permission from the publisher, except in the case of brief quotations embodied in
critical articles and reviews.

ACKNOWLEDGMENTS

"At the Mental Ward," "The Disease," "The Letter M," "The Walls," and "The
Hot Violet Sapphic Martyr to Her Hot Pink Daughters" appeared in *(Dis)
Integration* in 2017.

Jessica would like to thank everyone who has supported her and her work,
especially after January 2017. She extends her sincere gratitude to those who
have supported the publication of this collection of poems. Special thanks to
Finishing Line Press, Kathleen Bryce Niles, David Sherman, Lee Zimmerman,
Jackie Nasso Cooke, Michael Rembis, Michael Rutter, and Andrew Sacks.

Publisher: Leah Maines
Editor: Christen Kincaid
Cover Art: Lee Zimmerman
Author Photo: Vincent Lopez - www.vincentlopezphotography.com
Cover Design: Jackie Nasso Cooke

Printed in the USA on acid-free paper.
Order online: www.finishinglinepress.com
also available on amazon.com

Author inquiries and mail orders:
Finishing Line Press
P. O. Box 1626
Georgetown, Kentucky 40324
U. S. A.

Table of Contents

For Dar and Elan.

*In honor of
Rose Pyne Walsh.*

"The problem is not that we're voiceless; it's that we're not heard."

Viet Thanh Nguyen

Doors

The first doors most of us know are hospital doors,
we hear the buzzing, clueless that it is a signal to us
that we are being shuttled through, allowed to pass, perhaps
we see a red light, mixed meanings we cannot decode,
we will see red and not know, from the comfy confines
of our carriers, in the crimson blur, that to enter is also
to exit; before we read, we hear a forearm strike a bar,
or we are detected and the door opens without our arms.

Doors then cannot be closed for years for fear of tiny fingers
that might become caught or squeezed, and crumbled,
so if locks cannot be deployed then through the peephole
in the gates we learn to study with intense and obstructed vision
what it means to be on the other side, and we grow to see
over the edge, to glimpse a grander spectrum of the view,
or, if we don't, we learn to climb, and then begin to note
windows and doors, curtains and knobs, in the distance.

And then some of us are ushered through the open doors
of education, unless we are not white enough, not privileged
enough, *we who are not enough* to enter freely have to bang
on the door; we then have to gather together and hold the trunk
of a wounded tree destined for paper but not for our ink,
and we have to ram it against the iron, nicking the locks,
until something busts in us and we storm the library inside,
open all the books and files, repossess the folders and volumes
wherein all of our narratives have been erased and banned.

We occupy doorways, line stairwells, file into halls, afraid
that as soon as we leave, new doors meant only for closure
will be erected, if we rest even for a moment, we may never be
permitted in again, but if we demand acknowledgement through
occupancy, there is always the threat that we will be kept in,
that we will be books closed, our cabinets slammed, our traces painted
over with glue, that we will be sealed, that we will be shut.

A door is never a choice; a door is a catch, a latch: we enter
or we leave, according to an order machine, a machine, we never stop
to think about doors until they lock us in, until we are pinioned,
facing them, straining against restraint, until we equate the red alarms
set on our departures with the inner alarms of forced entry.

Nightgowns

Two small children in flimsy nightgowns,
under soft yellow sheets, unknowing, sleeping
somewhere else, thank God, anywhere else,
in any room, other than the one next to mine;

my children in their beds, far away
from the room deafened, the room rattling,
the room creaking, the room buzzing,
the room bleeding white sterility, next to me,

the woman without teeth, whose hair
in shreds and chunks hangs helplessly,
this vicious mouse, this woman of Meth,
who I cannot actually see but can hear move:

her clamor paralyzes me, from approach
to approach, she tries to reason, resorts
to begging, then unleashes Sycorax, tearing
her doctor apart to no effect, her primitive captivity

pounds in my chest and the guillotine
of predicament arrives; she is smothered
in sterility before she is abandoned, chopped,
the body responds when it is locked in a box
the body responds, it attacks the walls,

it seeks electric outlets, hooks, toothpicks,
paperclips, pencil tips, it looks out into the world
death-bound, a morbid hound unleashed
that would rather be dead than lose its liberty,

I cannot escape the rooms attached to mine,
I cannot escape the woman, I hear her bashing,
her body revolting, I hear her cursing, spitting,
unloosing her toothless bombs, her head against

slabs of shame; I hear her demanding death, and think,
this woman unleashed, wrinkled and freezing
under a backless nightgown, was once a child,
lead her back to bed, to soft yellow sheets, to sleep.

Lavender Fertility

I must speak into the void
of my own
        abnormality,
and hope
    that its echoes
            will be heard beyond
its oppressive chambers,

will reverberate through

the hollow roots
of indifferent valleys
and malicious galleys

until they reach the highest
mountain of proliferation

and there speak with a cadence
so oxygenating

that it clears
the fog, with words so full

of the particles of truth

that each letter is a billion seeds
of vision

turning snow to rain, enriching
soil,

promising
    lavender reckoning,
    a fertile Spring.

Occupational Therapy

You can't play a harp in prison
but they let you bang on a drum;
in fact, if you don't bang on a drum
you will be considered defiant, ornery,

so I tap on a drum, but I long
for a harp, for a violin, for my funeral
song; I cannot muster enjoyment,
so I feign opacity, neutrality, gentility,
at the thumps and jangles of humiliation,
pretending to be soft, pretending.

For a good report you have to sing
their songs, regurgitate, assimilate,
a smile will get you far, as far as your
next dose, compliance is the only
measurement of wellness, when your paper
trail is your paper trial, is all you are; a group of middle

-aged women cock their heads sheep
dog style, looking to place a check
in the box that says you seemed happy,
your meds must be working, the funding
will keep coming, the program will continue

doing its job.

Sonnets from the Psych Ward

do not exist. Nobody in the psych ward
is writing a sonnet,
          nobody is writing
                    anything.
      Writing is not allowed
in the psych ward unless
you are being asked
to write your name on the dotted line

that will sign away your right
after right after right,
              those ineffable
(you thought inalienable)

               signs of humanity
that you do not know you have
until you find out, too late:
            they were taken
when your keys were taken,
when your purse was taken,

you won't need this, you won't need that,

    you won't need

anything
because you do not exist.

Sonnets are not something you write,
or even contemplate, in the psych ward,

unless you are there for over
ninety days
unless you are there forever
(and of course you will be)

unless you are forced to hallucinate
the sonnets writing themselves
on the walls, on the walls, on the walls,
or that

Shakespeare is in the room next to yours,
   also bound up, also without ink.

Psychiatric Room Sonnet

A man will walk his way from room to room,
To him they are just paths he cannot tread;
He'll speak in tongues of demons in each bed,
And curse about a wife who left her groom;
I'll hear him from the deepest dregs of doom.
Oh there they are: the tears I cannot shed,
I'll cringe, am I the living or the dead?
Sanity is cruel but beats these meds.
I'll lose my sense of darkness and of light.
The moon is fake, the system breeds such shame.
They say I am lame, but only in the brain.
The nurse at the pill bar lines up the next flight,
She says I've been too wild and too tame.
Who needs eyes when there's no morning light.

Straight Jacket

Yanked out
   of the womb of the 80s, we were grabbed
up, put under spotlights, wiped with towels,
                       and wrapped
in white blankets, corner to corner, tucked
away, our blood in a bath

like squirming burritos from Hell,
                      jailbreak limbs
unable to move,
helter skelter turning inward,

          we came out

and heard for the first time

our rebel scream,   primal,
unending, while our mothers' bodies laid
enslaved, engorged: with them

   we shared a dissipating
hormonal wavelength that would multiply;
                   hers was ours
and now ours was to be hers for all time,
a syncopation of being
that no cut cord would ever be able to sever,
a commotion no strap would be able to bind,

          we were

born, our limbs were tucked, our legs were crossed,
some of us lost
               appendages, we were cut,
our arms were bent, our parts were counted,

our missing parts, accounted,
we were tethered in loving, fearful obligation,

into convention,
and our fathers
would scorn us for we were not
appreciative, and
        we would scorn our fathers
for not wanting to listen, for not waiting to listen
to all we had to say, to scream, we did not coo,
we could not, we did not giggle,
we did not
            settle; we spit up and gurgled
like gorgons, our eyes bulging out
of our heads, turning
                our doctors to stone,
we did not want this blanket, this whiteness,

this separation

:   to be cast off into a world of unbelonging,
to be thrown in a crib of complacency,
and so we went on a sleep strike,
        stayed up all night and shook the bars,
we kept them up, we stole the hours,

we never slept, never straightened,

never got that look of bloated dismay
off our ungrateful faces, never stopped pissing

and moaning, we were never straight,
we would find our way
out of this jacket

our will, our choice
    to live unstrapped
                lives of disgrace.

It is January 20th

The doctor is calling.

She says to you,
        without saying,

tell me what I want
to hear,
verify the hastiness
of all my generalizations,

the quick imprecise
diagnoses
and the bias-based

confirmations,

verify the invented fears

tell me I better keep her
Locked in. Here.

You take the doctor's call,
you freeze in the terror

of your own guilt,
of your bystander error;

you tell her
what she wants to hear,

keep it short,
keep it simple, keep it false

while my life, my liberty,
hang on the line.

You say, without saying:

doctor,
we were afraid,

(doctor,
keep her locked away).

The Existence of Green

We had no need
for the existence
of blue, we were
given gray and told
to obey, granted
black and white,
we were denied
color other than
fluorescence,
we were denied
life, we had no need
for courtesy,
or questions,
we had no need
for explanations,
we had no need
for the existence
of green.

Daybreak

Something broke inside me that day
I acquired every disease known and unknown,
I died every death it is possible to die,
I broke every bone, fractured every part,
clogged, twisted, contorted, exploded,
my genes mutated, I became an XYZ
I became an LGB, I became a T;
something broke inside me that night
but there was nothing left
inside me to break after that day
so I assume it was day itself that broke
and now I survive on the memory of hope.

What It Means to Surrender

It is not that you do not have hands,
it is not that you do not have mouths,

it is that you know

that if you scream you will lose
the ability to produce sound, you know

instinctively that you must live in lost
echoes, that any movement is suspect,

and that the absence of movement is suspect,
you know if you cry you die, you give in,

you know if you make fists, even feeble
fists, they will be strapped with leather;

it is that you know

there is no way, in or out, no way
at all, there are only the inches between

your shoulders, between your hips,
the saliva you hate to swallow down,

there is only the collapse of bones,
the implosion of organs, the muscles

straining but stuck, quiet but not too quiet,
you must speak but not on your own

behalf, you must breathe, you must close
your eyes when it is time, and open

to a world without end that is also dead,
to an end without world that is also alive,

it is not that you do not have nerve,
it is not that you do not have sense,

it is not that you do not have the urge
to fight or flight, and fight again,

it is not that you do not recognize
the end of times when it arrives,

it is not that you do not have humanity,
it is not that you do not inwardly rise;

it is that you know

The Collar and The Leash

Whenever we see the collar and a leash,
we see ourselves
bent, in the undead of snowless

winter, leaving

a disappearing trail
    pressing down with purpose
into the gravel   of our rejected triviality,
hoping to scrape a plea, to have the lost
skin be seen,

       crawling down

the street yielding to a dictator
whose name is on repeat, who kicks us
as he pleases, with his gavel-shaped boot,
in the midst of those too scared to look
let alone to show a hint that they disapprove,
and from down here
in the revelry of reproach,
our entire casing becomes loose
and we are exposed:

      we are girls stripped down to red

    from neck to toe, girls whose heads
        were knocked with clubs,
     girls who have to hide our brains
       behind our knees, dragged
          along streets of
    a collective conscience ceased,
whenever we are in a man's collar,
      attached to his leash,

    we see ourselves

not needing knees, ourselves detaching
our heads, beyond his reach,
ourselves growing spikes and wings
ourselves flying higher,

as high as it takes, to be.

Psych Ward Cinderella

The sweetest soul possessed the sweetest insanity,
she danced merrily along the floors of squalor and saw
a paradise, she asked for a broom and she swept,
a satisfied Cinderella, she sang, and we were her birds
and bees, in a dream, for she was no longer homeless,
no longer left to roam the streets, she preferred
the safety of the institution, a place where she could
wrap herself in a white sheet and close her eyes
and not be raped, where her back of invisible scars
would not be scraped, she taught me perception
is a paradox in which we are all trapped, homelessness
made Hell seem like home, she had been awake
for too long, like a smashed clock on the pavement,
the plastic blocks felt like cushions, pig slop seemed
gourmet, she raised up her hands, while I watched from
my bed in horror and wonder, and she gave thanks.

No Exits, No Calls

And the song
of this chaos plays
in a quartet of strange,
a few notes between
minor and major,
held long
reaching into an eternity
of the heart,
and in a moment
I am with you,
the happiest smile
of my life,
the one I wish
my daughters could know,
the one ripped from
the womb of the sunflower
of my happiness in bloom,
the song is cut short,
the melody torn
from the instrument,
the holes in the flute
gagged, the strings snipped,
the voice choked,
and the smile
that is my life fades
the moment we stop
traveling together,
the moment
my daughters are told
I am in the hospital
and cannot leave,
and cannot call,
all thunder muted,
all rain stopped,
all tin roofs covered
in blankets of death
when the silence
of this chaos takes over

Washcloths

When you are entered
into
    a psychiatric camp,

the warfare is chemical,

the towels are abysmal,
the washcloths
       are locked away,

you have to be escorted

to your washcloth

by one of the ones
    in the dog-paw scrubs
     who holds the keys

to the fate
of your laughable hygiene—

you have to wait
and wait
    and   wait:

your body shrinks
to fit the towel,

your spirit is scraped,

your chest
       collapses

and the diluted orange
soap slides
off

but never the shame

The End of Dry Erasure

There was a reason I chose a permanent marker
when I wrote on the surface of my bedroom wall:
I did not want to be erased, did not want to be easy
to wipe away, like something water-based, or chalk.

I am guilty of having a soul that seeks a permanence;
remember the billboard, remember the rooftop,
remember the paper, the doorway signs, remember you
decided, from your mind, it would be better to erase me.

Oh but you could not—for from inside you, I multiplied,
became inanimate, became the board, became the flag,
became the leaking pen in your hand, became the things
you could not ignore, wash, disassemble, or hide.

Your thought, your chisel, your shadow, your friend,
your keeper of fractured time, I became ineffable,
I became the antithesis of deletion, the metamorphic,
I became the beginning and the end of dry erasure.

Put Away

You put away socks,
not people

unless you want to
bury them.

How did I get here?
Was it for being gay?

My mother
used to threaten me

with psychiatric
punishment

because I was
(the target of hate)

she said she could
have them take me

away.

I thought I escaped
only to find

the ones I trusted
in place of my mother

would wait many years
and then enact her

threat—a decade

under the dining room
table, words shrieked

into my soul, looming,

what she said was true:

in this day and age
I could be put away,

would be put away

for being gay.

On Becoming a Goodwill Bag

Don't bring me anything I would want
to wear, to use,
when I am released,

       when I am revived.

Whatever I wear in here is going
                  to be etched
in the dregs of my mind, a reminder

of when I was trashed,
of when I was trash,
of trash.

So bring me trash, and only that.

I want to wear the worst of the worst
while I am here:

the mismatched socks, the ones with holes,
the too-short pants with baggy,
               broken knees.
Bring me the worst you can find,
bring me old torn up sweats, and tees
you have shoved into bags
        in the garage.

You don't need to bring me clothes,

not from my closet,
       not from any closet,
clothes were something worn
by the person I was before

        I became trash.

That was the past, this is now
I am at your mercy,
a thing put in bags,

just bring me whatever you find
                lying around

To Tear The Woman From The Page

Since when did a woman deep
in thought become a danger,
a viable threat to society, and when
did a woman laughing cause
"grown" men to shit in their pants,
and when were her pupils the target
of a low-class, shoddy investigation,
since when did a woman lost
in herself, writing new languages,
warrant a warrant and remediation,
since when did Emily Dickinson
go from being paranoid at the window,
above the trees, seeing phantoms
in the leaves, to sitting in a cloud
of surveillance, since when did her desk
become a criminal object and her
pen a weapon, since when did fully
-armed men in buckled-hats
go back in time to lock down her thoughts,
force medicate the volumes
out of her imagination, censor
the poet from experiencing her own
genius, condemn the body of work
to desecration, since when
did a fascist flare up result in a plan
to destroy Dickinson, and any future
reincarnations, from the inside out,
pulling paper from her hands, sending
her on a vacation to a room without
a window, indefinitely, since when
did literacy pose a threat so blatant
to masculine authority that men with guns
and bullet-proof vests had to administer
violations, had to muffle and mute her
incantations, bruise her with defamation,
had to tear the woman from the page,
to make visible her invisible chains,

to make invisible her visible claims,
to steal the solitary study of a woman
whose madness would not be contained?

Grider Street

I remember when the walls screamed,
I remember when the walls bled,
I remember when the walls shook,
I remember the walls of cement.

I remember when the walls stood,
separating each of us in our coffin beds,
I remember when we were our rooms,
I remember when we were our beds.

I remember when we were the walls,
when our screams were ignored,
how our ducts were torn from our tears,
how our tears surrounded our pickled heads.

I remember when the walls were silent,
I remember when the echoes spread,
I remember when the walls were chains,
I remember all the streaks of pain.

I remember when the walls moaned,
I remember when the walls groaned,
I remember when the walls were soft
but the builders of the walls were stone.

I remember when the walls were crumbling,
I remember when the walls were foam,
I remember when the walls were fire,
I remember when we were the walls,

I remember the walls of our broken home.

What We Smuggle to Survive

for Lucy Winer

The eyes of the tranquil, the eyes of the tranquilized
lull my wide, drooping soul into the refuge of a sigh,
across the table, across the desks, across the auditorium,
across the prison, across the institutions of life,
she tilts her head, hers is a language of breath,
and I have never spoken like this. I am overtaken,
the perfunctory slides away, I am taken
by a stillness, she breathes me into a place where I don't need
to explain, where I can rest, where it is possible
to surrender and not be usurped by surrounding.
The dish in front of me is covered in pearls,
soft, they fill my mouth, and something gentle
is on the horizon, it seems, rising over the rim
of a bottle cap lens, the tranquility of defeat,
the sharing of a holy silence at a meal. She gives
in one breath twenty years of institutionalization,
twenty years of speaking into a vacuum, where even
the announcement of a loss of voice is lost, her muted
voice finds me, speaks to me, drowns out every other
thing; I take it in, I'm taken by it, I bring it home,
I take it across borders, across decades, with me,
aware that we are sailing a reckless psychotropic sea,
aware of what we smuggle to survive.

My Cord

You broke my vacuum cord
and I shrieked and condemned you to
sweep out the chimney of your sooty soul,
and then I swore and stomped, and implored

the cord to retract, and then I collapsed
on the floor, beside the cord, and wept and wept,
cord in hand, cursing you and the gods, I had

one object of quality, one single machine
that I possessed, a portable red Kenmore,
a vacuum, now broken, now no more,
you cried with me over the broken

cord, you let the tears spill into
your Leon Trotsky spectacles, you stood
above me in your wool coat, a child
trembling in the presence of a militant

reprimand, a mind without memory,
as I pounded the coffee-stained gray
carpet and shook for I had lost

my daughters, my everything,

my cord

Problem Children of the Lightning War

I am a problem child,
a miscreant, a delinquent,
I am a child
      with a problem,
and a child with the
     fiery will
to expose it,
   to unfold it,
I am a problem
        child,
I do cause trouble
     and mayhem,
I do stand up when others sit,
I do rebel
when they submit,
      I do talk back
    when faced
with punishment.
I will admit, I am a problem
child,
    there is never a time
when I don't speak
      out of turn,
nor I will ever learn
from a PTA
also known as   The Blitz,
  when lessons come
from the ends of cannons
or the frayed edges
     of   whips,
I am a problem child,
a haughty
    problematic child,
and I encourage you
        to survive
like St. Paul's survived,
to sound your problem cry,

              to guard the gates
of the cathedral
        of problem children,
to
be a problem child, too.

A Wild Exile

I hear her wailing, the woman without a name,
her feeble arms outstretched, her wrists together,
the frame of a heart, as with ethereal handcuffs,
waiting for a virgin bouquet, she braces herself,

beholding her own heart, she begs to be uprooted
from the court, to live and die flammable, a skeleton
donning a paper doll dress, on her knees, to be holy,
delivered from the waste bin of broken ideals,

her prayers are forced back into her mouth,
her thoughts are shut up in her head, she is sealed
in the echo chambers of denied translation,
they refuse to speak her language, they use their own

to condemn her,

but all understand the language of the gavel,
when it comes down before a fair trial, the table
of justice cracked as she strains her voice, her lungs
stretch, her valves burst, the nurses, the aides,

and the guards stand around, hearing her unsound
sounds but not one can interpret the soul, not one
listens or considers the cries of the woman
wailing, turning inward, like the sepsis of the spirit,

and there, inside the silent screen of unending
asylum, I catch the blessed disease of her agony,
the clean air of a new consciousness, I implore her
across the carpet to infect me with a righteous rally

cry of disobedience,

all the while, I play the part of regretful miscreant,
cling to my resources, use privilege to wrangle

release, but I am bound to the woman without a name,
bound to her plight, for she is thrown into a chair,

she is strapped down, and she is wheeled out
of the building, rolled back into a bus, across town,
up four floors, through locked doors, into a chemical tomb
where they sedate the hell out of her until she protests

no more, while I reap the guilt, my conscience
acquiring new shackles, an illusion of freedom, the knowledge
that my survival was a fluke, I vow to be two places
at once, I conjure the ghost of her riled subjugation,

her fleeting uprising,

I try to bring her back, to give her more
than muted wailing, than defeat, to catch her
when she slumps over, to look into her bloodshot eyes,
to stir with solidarity the melting pot of our identities,

every last ounce of myself, I commit to the woman
without a listener, without a name, without a language,
whose protests were drugged out of her, I fall
to my knees to live beside her perpetually,

to breathe her own fire back into the vessel of her
squandered humanity, to remind her collapsed wings,
to unbuckle the belt and scream, now is time to join,
to fight, to ascend, outstretched and open, into

a wild exile.

Where The Lilacs Stood

We hid ourselves on the high shelves,
we locked ourselves in the locked lofts,
we hid ourselves in the closed trunks,
in the closets, we were lilacs lost.

I hid myself in your book bags,
I placed myself on your blank page,
I hid myself in your nightstand,
in your closet, with your sage and jade.

You hid yourself in my bed sheets,
You veiled yourself in my ink stains,
You hid yourself in my heartbeats,
in my garden, where the sun still reigns.

We found ourselves in the lilied wood,
we planted ourselves on the green stage,
we found ourselves where the lilacs stood,
in the garden, with our jade and sage.

Until His Domination Dies

I will never hold my peace,
I will speak now, now, and now,
and ever, and now, again, I will detonate
in perfect beauty, like a mad pearl
in a too-tight oyster, and I will not hold
the illness of the buffoon groom
in anything but contempt,
I am stained, my heart, singed,
my eyes, tinted, I see through
glasses colored by your sins,
in war paint, the peace I will not hold
is riotous, fragments of recognition
explode, tainting every bleeding steak
you paid someone
to slice, every glass of wine
is chipped with the smiling
teeth of each and every dummy
nodding with his fist in their heads,
while I stand and make my speech,
of riot, *and let us all raise a fist*
and drink to a mouth broken to bits,
to marry that which you hate:
isn't it bliss? Their glasses become
half full with his piss—swish,
tell everyone, especially your father
this: *your closet is coming*
with you,
I am that abyss—I open myself
of my own volition
and invite inside all the perplexed
————guests,
sit down and learn,
before she becomes the urn
with his ashes on her rim
who gave you the fold,
who made you the blind,

I wash their eyes, *welcome*
to the closet, come inside,
where the objection in abjection resides,
we object against the objectionable
on the altar of sacrilegious sacrifice,
contemptuous malignancy,
cuckolded cock of complete idiocy,
I will not hold my peace
until the heterosexual man's dream
of dominion falls off the cliff
of his own impotence,
until his domination dies.

A Chaos that is Universal

The past is not behind me, it is here.

With me, undertow into undertow,
at all moments I am in the whirlpool

of a deficient living company, always
so unkind in its delivery of kindness,
rather like pieces of the liquid puzzle

of what we've lived, one that nibbles,
unconvinced, before it swims into
another net, not seeing the net's gaps
into the rubbery rubbish of release's

impenetrability. I do not live denied
by denial; instead I bite into her, stifled
in the wicked presence of the elusive;

instead I spin, I swim in an aquatic
tank of time lost, time that is full of sass
and devoid of industry, all sharp hands
and borders, and orders, scattered

into wisdom's abyss, into a frenzy
of desire, my suffering laugher, wands
of surrender that I've held underwater

sinking with my stone life vests, hysteric
longing, a need so agonizing it pleasures:

all are debris in a landscape into which
we have been tossed, into some greater

consciousness, the arrows, the fish,
and the anchors, all are one and I am one

particle of a chaos that is universal.

The White Lie Moon

In your closet
there was a bed
chained to a floor
and a girl chained
to the bed and I
was the girl chained
to the bed and you
were the chain link
hallucination
of the moon
at the chain-linked window;
you not quite
fluorescent
as I watched you,
your indifference
and your indecipherability,
I held you there,
for a moment, thought
about what you meant
to me before the clock
stopped, and then
I learned to be
indifferent
to my own heart
but I was never able
to be indecipherable
like you— the moon
would always allude,
and I would learn
in an instant, to be
a cog in a man's machine
of lies, a whipped
metal cog,
just doing my part
in his telling of time,

I looked at the window,
it wasn't the moon
I was seeing,
it was a deadly white lie.

We Hold Our Exiled

We are in an era of emancipation-mocked, in which the mockery
masks the villainy so much that we cannot see the harm,
so now we depend on the radicals, on those with internal scars,
those trampled deepest in our mud, to write a way out of this,

we write in subcultural textualities, we write where tyranny cannot
find us, our stanzas are hidden in virtual passageways,
invisible to the patriarchal eye, our stories cannot be read,
our meanings not understood, by anyone whose default mode
is to patronize, to criminalize whatever challenges the authority
of illiteracy; we were poets before they called us mad,

before they had us followed, before they had us led
into deathtraps, before they sought to lock us into misogyny,
and its most violent fantasies, we were artists speaking truths,
we were who we were, and we were free on the canvas and page,

but now even the trees are marked, anything green placed under
arrest, but now we determine to grow stronger than a chainsaw,
but now we hide our poems in our hearts, but now we memorize
each other in the blindness and learn to see through the unsaid,
in shadows cast over our soul's monuments, in harbors shut down—

the docks of integration, of intelligence, roped off, we leap
our way, faith or no faith, into the poisoned water and we swim,
whether we learned how or not, with our lips sealed, we swim
as if we're beyond human, we hold our exiled

words in our pregnant bellies, we swim the never-ending ocean,
we swim so far out we cannot see a shore, we can see nothing
but our vision of welcome, and we are a school darting in synchronicity,
anchored to a pink horizon only we see, where colors meet
and are safe, where the language and light are one, where

our reminiscences of horror are safe to take shape, where our voices
are not doomed to violence, we adapt as we are escorted out

and displaced from homeland:
we belong to the ocean and refuse the boat, into something more powerful
we travel, into a righteous oblivion beyond borders and walls.

At the Mental Ward

Come into the shower
at the mental ward
the smell of shit in the drain
at the mental ward
crouch under the stream
at the mental ward
water trickling, hydro dripping
pressure lacking, nurses laughing
like a mouth that's dribbling
at the mental ward

Come into the shower
at the mental ward
sorry but there's no hot water
at the mental ward
use your washcloth as a towel
at the mental ward
pick up the orange liquid
with the yellow duck sticker
and squeeze

Come into the shower
at the mental ward
silverfish are scooting
on the grimy floor
no one cares if you're clean
at the mental ward
no one cares if you scream
at the mental ward
you will never be seen
at the mental ward

I showered every day
at the mental ward
hung my head low
under the broken faucets
at the mental ward

shivered and refused to feel
at the mental ward
not my body, not my mind
at the mental ward

I'm home in my shower
but I'm still at the ward
those are silverfish tears rushing
from my showerhead
I have hot water here
but I'm still shivering
at the mental ward
I can scrub all the walls
and wipe the floors
but I'm sane enough to know
I'll still be in the shower
at the mental ward

The Walls

Are they still after you,
are they still threatening
you with knives,
the walls,
Are they still beating
you to a pulp,
the walls,
Are they still sawing
at you, toe by toe,
the walls,
Do they ever let up,
the walls,
do they ever take a nap,
the walls,
do they ever say nice things,
offer to carry your books,
offer to call you a taxi,
bring you a blanket, a cuppa,
with love,
The Walls,
tell you a childish joke,
the walls,
do they ever ask you what you think,
the walls,
do they always come
with a side of pills and a staff
of nameless nurses who smoke
six packs a day so they can nod
when you say things to
the walls,
who are you to
the walls, the tormentors:
we know who they are to you
Billy, Jenny, Hey You,
but to the rest of us
when the walls start talking,

everything else is stripped away:
all but the walls

and you

The Hot Violet Sapphic Martyr
to Her Hot Pink Daughters

Do not blame my death on belief;
I died because I chose to speak

In shifting, blurring, amped up hues,
crossing lines of pink and blue

I died for holding neon hope,
impenetrable by killers in white coats

Whose iron bars were fastened
to my body but nothing to my soul

Its immortal song is a lighthouse, a burning lilac
flame of faith, an elevated island remote,

A pillar of resistance that stands afloat,
blazing yet safeguarded from harm

I bled, I'm gone but love won't rest,
it burns and resounds as your shield

I died a Sapphic martyr's death, a hot violet
mind, I died, your mother, colorful and bright,

Policed to death, assess-inated
by primitive animals, earthly slime,

Honor your will to live and be heard,
trust your minds and use your words

Your revolutionary mother was sentenced
for committing purple crimes in her chest,

Bury your mother in a casket of truth,
in the opal cloaks and foam daggers of youth,

And always know when she fought, from pastel
pink to black and blue, it was for you

The Disease

They want to extract
my system of belief
like a cancerous tumor;

they were so close
to implanting illness
in the flora of my mind;

they might have made
me twitch for the rest
of my life but the belief

is me, is mine, is what
will outlive my end
of times: there is no cure

for (the disease
of) hope— for (the disease
of) humanism—

I have seen too many
high-paid homicidal
quacks in coats and robes

charged with saving bodies,
not lives, injecting a world
of pretend, pharmaceutical

extermination, into our arms
and asses: we, 21st Century lab
rats, we the nutjobs and shitbats;

they tried to cure me
by taking away my liberty
and killing my will to live

but my will grew, my allegory
turned to armor, my allegiance
to my truth spread; I escaped

and now the contagion of hope
holds the pen, writes the diagnosis,
prescribes the disease.

Justice's Hands

Those are the perils of taking justice
into your own hands: there will be callouses,
there will be nails, holes, rivers, and choirs,
illuminated like constellations
under a microscope, bloody stars,
there will be showers of misinformation,
meteors of contradiction battling in the back
pocket of the universe's indifference,
there will be overturned steeples, the tongues
of bells to climb, there will be perils
in the hands that demand the change of times.

Chopsticks to the Mouth

These criminal objects, these chopsticks
from the devil, this comedy of insinuation

that you take to be realism in insinuatory
error, this parody of imaginary sushi,

this theatre of the doubly absurd
that you cast into the prison of literalism,

I bring the chopsticks to the crotch
and I bring the chopsticks to the mouth,

once more, don't you see, it is teen
rebellion, the desire to touch the hot stove

of my forbidden desire, because I have
been told an eyebrow no, beaten with silence

into a delectable chopstick insanity,
because I have cried too many useless tears

to the large of your back—a wall in the bed,
barricading me from pleasure, for too long,

I cannot wake you from your indifference
to my incandescent mind, but I can turn

to the shackles around me, get out of bed
after midnight, look for tools in the master's

cupboards, build myself an artillery
in my imagination, create an underground

of domesticity, I can sneak into the silver
ware drawer when you are at work,

and take the chopsticks to the mouth,
once more, to make you sick

instead of content in your status quo
of slumber, I am dead to you

except in your disgust, your diagnostic
reflux, if Bjork had done the same she

could have been your hero in her artistry
but you are a cabinet closed—*love yourself,*

you tell me as you refuse to love me,
love yourself and then you will no longer desire,

love yourself but never love yourself so much
you start making jokes about being the food

no one will eat, love yourself so someday
I can diagnose you with narcissism,

by all means love yourself, you say to me,
without words, day by day, and then you leave,

I go to your drawers, I take out the cheap
chopsticks, I make them magic, I make them

wands, I make myself relief, I move
the chopsticks, how strange I must be,

with only chopsticks, to learn to love
myself completely.

The Letter M

stands for Madness, righteous feminist madness,
the bloody mess, the seal of the oppressed, our screaming
voices beaten into silence, submitting to the will
of man, our feeble fists hitting the yellow walls,
our snapping wrists scraped by his legal papers, trapped
under his clutch, waiting for ages in a stone cell, a cuff,
opening the tomb of women's history, and raising itself again,

centuries of guilty consciences draining into our cauldrons,
bubbling with our prophetic muted, mutilated pasts, rising
out of the gunk of primordial patriarchy, hegemony written
in erasure, like restraints over, our histories, stories dug
into the ground, arms twisted like twigs until our hands
release the pens, our roots gather and plot
and we shoot up like hoards of angry daffodils in the cemetery
of the universe, the lion losing his place, the kingdom: its king,
the doctor: his authority, the officer: his gun, the judge: his gavel,

the M stamped on our heads becomes our emblem,
our superpower, we, seared with injustice, who learned to see
from its lens, we light fires in the attics of ourselves, and we jump
into annihilation's liberation, we rid the courtrooms, the hospitals,
the jails of the instruments of domination, we fill them
with our uncooperative bodies, we fill them with our voices, our choruses,
our cacophonies, our hysterias, our shrieks, our flowing ink wells,
our volcanic pens, our notebooks, our printing presses, our letter Ms.

I Am Alive

I will not know if it is raining,
if the earth shakes, if it cracks
in half, if it crumbles to nothing,
I will not know.

I will not know if it is blowing,
if the ice pelts, if the snow piles,
if the wind is full of wrath
if the blizzard of the century
takes hold of the city,
I will not know.

I will not know if it is burning,
if the street goes up in flames,
if the building boils away,
I will not know.

I will not know if my daughters
are crying, if they are in need,
if they are entertaining frightening
possibilities, if they are bullied,
if my daughters bleed and call for me,
I will not know.

But from in here, inside these walls of fear,
where no snow falls, where pounding
rain cannot persist, where flames devour
before you can steer clear, where daughters'
voices cease to exist,
I will know.

I will hear, I will touch, I will see
when my rights dissolve,
when I am rendered absolved
from the contents inside me,
I will call:

my child, I am not dead,
my child, I am alive,

and she will know.

Flower Drum Song

In the carcass of heteronormativity,
a shining violet flickers, holding in her petals
the tender streams of the sun, and it is my heart,
that light, that life, striving against all odds

and preferences, to exist; I feel myself a ribbon
lit at both ends, an implosion of undulation, aggrieved
with a moment's hope chasing ten years
of despair, for there are two different kinds

of fire, but neither expires, though someday she,
the beating violet, frail and ferocious,
in the void of half-decisions, will be called
all the things she is not, and ruled and overruled

a shadow, as the tunnels of death, manmade
gorges, and other inversions of reality, too,
are misidentified as orbs of gaslight cast on bridges
built over water that throbs with partitioned ice

and commoditized electricity, so the shock
of souls of wayward girls are mistaken for outages,
for blemishes, for smut, for unwanted day
or undesirable night, so are our lives flipped at switches,

rolled like dice on a rigged table, forced into escape
routes in search of paradise; this is how
we learn to be silken meteors and fearsome
flowers, how we take it upon our unrecognized bodies

to give birth to new botanic constellations,
to succulent twilights, this is how we feel
the wisdom of the cactus in our torn apart sides,
when she says: to be sharp is the way to be alive;

I disband from myself, I abandon belief, a woman
shrinking into her own disappearance above a well
of introspection, I will myself a lily pad, a leaf to cradle
my fragility—to remain a drowning violet, a scaled

back lily, sewing what the daffodil bid: that a carcass teems
with spiritual hymns, that one in a hostile plot
may disperse and die, but the trapped may also thrive;
I recall the tune to a song not-allowed, and I sing it aloud.

[And what if we are afraid of what we will become.]

A voice in me calls
and says: become

the things they most fear,

hold high the flags
they make you fold,

be the face of every disease
they seek to eradicate,

be the arm of every body
they wish to amputate,

be the voice of every woman
they force into silence,

be the pen for every hand
they try to bind,

be the missing limb
they will never find,

be the thought that every censor
seeks to remove;

a voice in me calls,
                and says:
become or you will lose.

—　　　　　—

The silence of others

occupies space,

immeasurable

space, not only in
my head and bed,
but on the streets,

in the alleys, in the

twelve-minute
  courtrooms.

The silence of others

it is the least safe

of all spaces,

lacks definition

except in hard
consequence,

shifts in shape
occupying injustice's

ever-present

interim

Monster Bloom

The girl has bloomed into a monster.

What does medicine do
to people who are not sick?

What does money do
to people who have too much?

What if the flower is overwatered?

Will the flower become a girl?

Will the girl wilt—arise from her wilting?

What does a flower-girl do
when she becomes a monster?

Will she growl? Will she bloom?

Will she be resigned
to live as a flower of containment,
an ornamental monster?

We Know Our Horizon

Done with walls,

we carve out doors and cast
ourselves

through the frames

into the rushing of truth,
we flood

the wine-dark final days, elude
the undercurrent, expel
the undertow,
we know

our horizon cannot be diluted,

and when from the chalice
we are excluded,

we join the channel *and flow*

Pupillary Fixation

I cannot call your name
or think your name
in the wake of shattered days

I cannot hear my own
name, can only cringe
to feel it vibrate in a vortex

of delinquency, what is this
light that now appears,
what am I when I am

in an incubator designed
for suffocation; I shun
the light, the sturdier

the walls, the more virulently
they cave,——ferociously
they crack,——suddenly

I become buried, am I no longer
permitted to exhale, the dark
of fluorescence casts cannons

into spiritual vessels I did
not know existed, I recognize
them as they obliterate,

I cannot study this light
when it has eaten me whole,
when I am under its hold,

I cannot earn high marks
when I am permanently marked
with institutional disapproval

all at once, at the close
of the soul, the eyes widen
and the sockets release them,

I can stop my sight but not
my vision, now the iris and pupil
are forced, into perpetuum, into

a state of constriction, condemned
to the end of dilation, fixed
luminance, sans absolution.

Sicily, Burning

There is nowhere to put this suffering,
I can't hide it in a bottom drawer
of myself, I can't throw it in a hat
before a crowd and make it disappear,
I cannot set my mind to rest, cannot
let the damage of the years scatter,
there is no where to place these fears ironed,
into me, this debris of sins unaccounted
for, the arrows in my sides from all
directions, there is no record
to set straight, my record has been
taken, stolen, claimed, revised,
while something else has been set
alive by fascist fire, tonight at a Red
Lobster, there was talk of Sicily,
the record burning, thousands of birth
records destroyed, the wiping out
of a people, and I am just one,
was just one, am no longer, am gone
before I am gone, such a long distance
from me is a moon blurred by a
failing vision, two hundred feet
from me is a post emitting the peach
light of its plight onto the street,
making black appear white,
and down below are two deer,
soundless, moving across the yard,
into each plot of unquestioned
destiny, but there is nowhere to put this,
this longing to be known on my own
terms, what is a moment of wit
against the burning of my future,
what is wishing that birth records
could reappear and death sentences
could be burned into nothing,

what is the bubbling of the soul
after midnight, hour by hour,
when no drawer exists to shut away
a train of thoughts, a trail of tears,
a chapter of suffering, what is the fire
inside me that burns alive all traces
of serenity, what is it that traps,
that straps, about burning memories
that live in us like lamps that cannot be
put out, what is it about a world
that burns birth records and with it
a people, what is it that opens all
the drawers in me and releases Mt. Etna,
but will not let the dead sleep.

I Am One

I am one of the violently mad ones
I am one of the rubber walled ones
One of the beaten and bruised ones
One of the starved and strangled ones
One of the David Star-stamped ones
One of the hanging from a tree ones
One of the down on her knees ones
I am one of the violently mad ones
I am one of the rubber walled ones

J e s s i c a   L o w e l l   M a s o n is a Ph.D. student and teaching assistant in the Global Gender and Sexuality Studies Department at the University at Buffalo. A writer, educator, and performer, Jessica has worked for Shakespeare in Delaware Park, Ujima Theatre Co., Just Buffalo Literary Center, the Jewish Repertory Theatre, and Prometheus Books. She has taught writing courses at Western Illinois University, Spoon River College, Carl Sandburg College, and Buffalo State College. Her scholarly interests center on women, literature, and madness. In 2014, Jessica was awarded the Gloria Anzaldúa Rhetorician Award by the Conference on College Composition and Communication. Some of her poems, articles, and reviews have been published by *Sinister Wisdom, Lambda Literary, Gender Focus, The Comstock Review, Diverse Voices Quarterly, Lavender Review, Wilde Magazine, IthacaLit, The Feminist Wire,* and *Praeger.* She is the co-founder of Madwomen in the Attic, a feminist mental health literacy organization in Buffalo, NY.

CPSIA information can be obtained
at www.ICGtesting.com
Printed in the USA
JSHW011701120919
1449JS00003B/7

9 781635 349979